The Hendricks Haiku Project II

Collected Poems from
Hendricks Avenue Elementary

Edited by George Foote

Silent E Publishing Company

Front cover by:
Ashley Nelson

Copyright © 2014 Silent E Publishing Co.

Silent E Publishing Company
4446 Hendricks Ave, #141
Jacksonville, FL 32207

ISBN–10: 1941091024

ISBN–13: 978-1-941091-02-9

1 2 3 4 5 6 7 8 9

Table of Contents

Foreword	5
First Grade	7
Second Grade	13
Third Grade	31
Fourth Grade	61
Fifth Grade	103
Faculty & Staff	123

Foreword

It has been five years since the original edition of "The Hendricks Haiku Project". The current students at Hendricks Avenue Elementary continue to excel in their academics and are ready for the chance to express creativity through poetry.

Japanese Haiku is our form of choice because readers and listeners can understand it easily. While these poems are not always easy to compose, the students at Hendricks, as you will see, continue to impress.

Haiku, for the purposes of this book, will be defined as a three line unrhymed poem with five syllables in the first line, seven syllables in the second line and five again in the third line, for a total of 17 syllables. The traditional haiku is also associated with nature and the seasons, often capturing a special moment that might otherwise be missed if the writer hadn't observed it. In the interest of creativity and fun, we also opened the subject matter up to sports, superheroes, food, hobbies, etc. It's my hope that you will enjoy the results.

Thanks to the staff, teachers, and parents for putting so much time, energy, and dedication into Hendricks Avenue Elementary. Thanks also to Principal Lacy Healy for her support of this and the many other programs that enhance the environment and educational experience here at Hendricks. Special thanks to the students for their participation in "The Hendricks Haiku Project II".

George Foote

April 2014

First Grade

Graceful Swans

Did you see the swan?
Swimming in the crystal pond
Gracefully gliding

Sofia West

Ants! Ants! Ants!

Ants work day and night
Ants carry ten times their weight
Ants are our class pets

James Cox

Trains

Trains are fun to watch
Big trains little trains long trains
Chugga, chugga, choo

Erik Willhide

Ten Candies

I have ten candies
Some spotted and some dotted
I ate them all up

Ella Hodgett

Fish

Fish are glimmering
In the big wide ocean light
Fish are swimming by

Beatrice Whitaker

Winter

It is getting dark
The trees are bare with snow
Lots of snow falling

Mahek Patel

Animals, Animals

I love animals!
Animals are such cute things
They are the best things!

Anna Nelson

Bella

Kittens are so cute
They snuggle and play a lot
I love my Bella

Gabrielle Shoraka

Soccer

Soccer is awesome
So, so awesome yes it is
I love to play it

Andersan Totty

African Animals

Some run, some slither
Some have horns, some have long trunks
I love them so much

Owen Betancourt

My Dog

I love you Hershey
You are my wonderful girl
My best friend, my dog

A.J. Sullivan

Second Grade

The Frog

The frog jumped the log
He landed on the wrong spot
He was not happy!

Fiorela Arevalo

Stinky Stuff

Do not smell a roach
It is kind of stinky, yuk
So don't smell a roach

Drew Williams

Love is in the Air

Love is in the air
There is love you cannot see
Love is everywhere

Tindell Harbin

No More Ice Cream

I don't have ice cream
I don't have it any more
'Cause it's on the floor!

Christopher Maloney

I love the Rain Storms

I love the rain storms
Not when it is everywhere
I love the rain storms

Katherine Cheshire

Weird Lizards

A lizard at dark
A weird fine line lizard yes
Oh yes he is weird

Liam Leonard

Resource

Art can get messy
Music is a melody
PE makes you strong

Tucker Ryan & Nico Allegretti

Noodles

Do you like noodles?
Noodly, doodly, do
I like noodles too

Madeline Hinchliffe

Horses

Galloping horses
In the desert hot and dry
Running to find food

Autumn Rose

Football Teams

Georgia, FSU
Cowboys, Seahawks, Patriots
I'm a football fan!

Parker Allred

Basketball

I like basketball
We made it to the finals
We lost by one point

Wil Holland

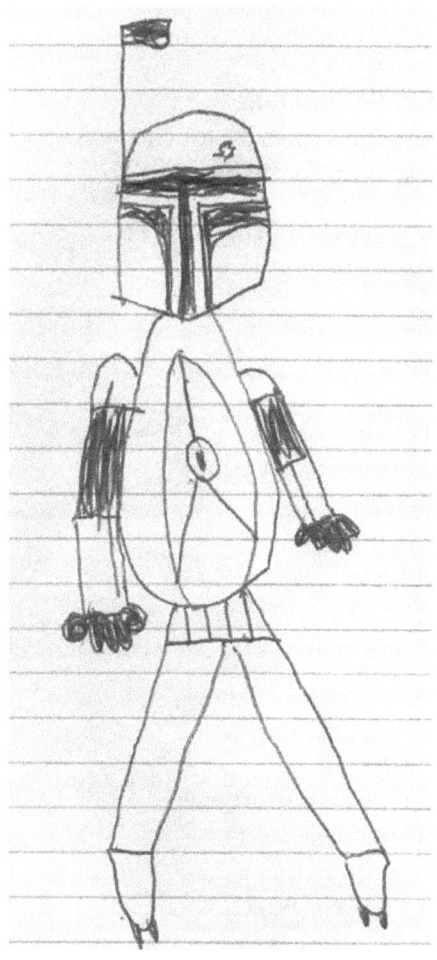

Boba Fett

Flew in the Sarlacc
Slayed the digesting Sarlacc
Made better armor

Quinn Gray

Jones-Drew

Jones-Drew likes to run
Jones-Drew likes to score touchdowns
Jones-Drew likes football

Gabriel Keiter

Hot Cakes

I love hot cakes yum
I love them very much yum
Better believe it

Gabby Wallace

Baseball

Baseball is very fun
Baseball is the best sport ever
Baseball is the best

Owen Selzer

Summer Coolin' All Day

Summer is so hot
You can go swim in the pool
You can chill all day

Brielle Smith

Lego Builder

I build with Legos
Colored blocks fit together
I build cars that go

Matthew Rohena

The Feeling of a Dolphin

I adore dolphins
Dolphins make me feel happy
They are beautiful

Ryn Rossi

Baseball

Baseball bats are swinging
Smells of spring are in the air
Peanuts on the ground

Tucker Ryan

Dancing

Dancing jumping fun
Twirling tapping sashaying
Jazz lyrical tap

Madison Ritchie

Swimming Fish

See their bright colors
Lickety-split they swim fast
It is wonderful

Tyler Grace Stein

Valentine

I love valentine
Valentine is time to greet
Valentine is sweet

Chloe Chaplin

Gymnastics

We swing on the bars
We fall off the long high beams
We miss our mill circles

Sarah Davisson

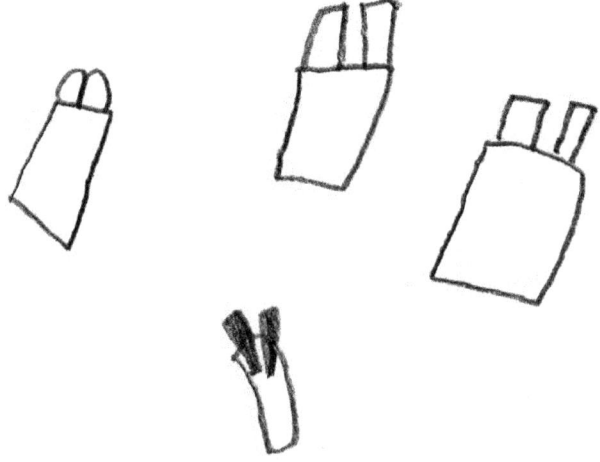

Legos

Legos, sitting still
A multitude of colors
I will play with them

Calvin S. Kenyon

Summer

My favorite thing
Swimming on a summer day
Playing with my friends

Isabella Kennedy

Summer Sun

Summer sun is bright
Warms the earth and makes me smile
Beautiful sun light

Leila Jane Davis

My Mom

My mom is so sweet
I know she is very kind
I really love her

Logan Marshall

Puppies and Dogs

I love all puppies
Big ones small ones dogs are fun
My pup is happy

Emiliano Makros

Bikes

Bikes are fun to ride
Because they go super-fast
I like my gray bike

James Mathis

Valentine

Valentine is fun
I love valentine so much
Valentine is fun

Elizabeth Roggenbuch

My Cats

I love cats so much
Cats can be very fluffy
Cats are super cool

Cali Jenkins

Butterflies Flying

Butterflies are cool
As they flutter through the air
Flitter, flutter, fly

Thomas Brandler

My Brother has a Skateboard

My brother crashes
My brother crashes to walls
I like him a lot

Sean Riggs

Summer

Summer is so hot
Summer is very rainy
Summer grows flowers

Jael Clark

Icee

Icee, so cold
Comes in many flavors
Blueberry is the best

Kaden Newman

My Brother has a Skateboard

My brother crashes
My brother crashes to walls
I like him a lot

Sean Riggs

Math Reflex

Oh my math reflex
I can play you day and night
I like you so much

Rivers Pearce

Jorden

Jorden likes baseball
Jorden likes to play baseball
Jorden likes baseball

Tyrell Cameron

Dogs

Dogs are animals
Dogs love humans very much
Dogs are awesome pets

Betty Leuthold

Cam is Boss

Cam is like a boss
Minecraft on my Xbox - yay!
Cam is so awesome

Cam Kettel

Skylanders

I love Skylanders!
Skylanders are so awesome!
Loads and loads of fun!

Evan Shakib

Rain

Do you like rain too?
How 'bout you, I like it too
So, do you like rain?

Madison Lee

A Nut in a Hut

A nut in a hut
He talks to everybody
Vacation he is

Gettys Smith

Third Grade

The Earth

We live on the Earth
The waves are calm and gentle
The sun is shining

Ellie Brown

Cute Baby Wolves

They eat bones and pork
They live with their family
Watch out for their teeth

Wallace Stine

Pandas

Pandas love bamboo
Pandas live in bamboo
Pandas are so cool

Sophia Benelbasry

Summer

Summer so much fun
So many fun camps and sports
It's just way too short

Riley Fluharty

Ice Cream is Good

Ice cream is so good
It's yummy and tasty great
Lick, lick, lick, lick, mmmm

Gavin Hill

Florida

Florida is cool
Florida is so awesome
Florida is cool

Darron Mccullough

Spring

Spring is very fun!
Spring is awesome and sunny
Spring is very cool!

Damian J. Wilson

The Dog on the Block

The dog on the block
Goes tweet, tweet, why would a dog
go tweet, tweet, what? hmm?

Ryker Tomberlin

Summer

Summer is play time
Summer is the time to swim
It is time to spend

Mason Terry

Fall

Beautiful colors
Jumping in leaf piles, so fun
Fall is really fun!

Kayla Wilcox

Sunshine

The sun is so bright
I love the sunshine a lot
The sun is awesome

Maddie Jefferies

Snow

The snow is so white
I want to play in the snow
I love the white snow

Kadence Burnett

Spring

Flowers bloom in spring
Spring is very amazing
Nature is awesome

Christine Kim

Minecraft

Minecraft is awesome
You can have fun playing it
That's why I love it

Malai Coffey

Games

Games are so awesome
Games are so cool and so fun
You should play some games

Ben Weiss

Minecraft

Minecraft is so fun
There are lots of mobs and tools
You craft, mine, and build

Thomas Brown

Summer

Summer is so bright
With lemonade and flowers
My favorite season

Elena Rankin

Flowers

Roses are red and
Violets are so, very blue
And tulips are pink

Nicholas Butcher

Baseball

Baseball is awesome
If you want to play sign up
Trust me you'll like it

Aston Brohl

My Friend

My friend is the best
My friend is always right on
He is a big mess

Mala Chi

Ice Skating

Ice skate ice skating
Ice skating ice Skating is
The best thing ever made

Nadya Hicks

My Dog's Fur

My dog is fluffy
Kind of, he is really scruffy
He is in the middle

Aidan Stephens

Labs

Like to play all day
Labrador retrievers rule!
Labs are really cool

Griffin Ranney

Summer Days are Great

It's hot and nice out
Go swim in the pool for cool
Summer days are fun

Annesia Graham

Football

Football is so fun
Football with friends is so fun
Football is awesome

Daniel Davisson

Gunter the Penguin

Gunter is so cute
Gunter really loves ice king
Gunter loves ice king

Addie Dandelake

Sun

Hot in the summer
So hot days I love to play
So much fun to play

Cameron Day

Pegasus

Pegasus flies high
All beautiful in the sky
With me on his back

Lily Guerrant

FLORIDA

Florida is nice
It has lots of beaches too
Florida is cool

Branden Solburg

The Sun

The sun is a star
To chill out your skin stay in
Just move and go, go

Enzo Antonio-Jose

Rajah

Rajah is the best
He is my favorite dog
He loves smelly bones

Gabe Wotton

Skies

Skies are beautiful
Cloudy or sunny or gray
Let's look at the sky

Nakya Jones

Hockey

Pucks go flying past
Hockey is so fun skating
Sliding is so fun

Ayden Taylor

Unstoppable Heroes

Invincible men
Stronger than one thousand men
Stronger than the sun

Marshall Brooks

Winter Days are Great

I am scared of bees
Winter days are so much fun
It is beautiful

Joseph Seamon

Butterflies

Butterflies are great
Better than ice cream or cake
Better than you, too

Thomas Sprague

Football

Throw, catch touchdown yay
Football is so fun to play
I'd play it all day

Jack Lunitz

Spring

Spring, spring I love spring
Because that is when the birds chirp
That's why I love spring

Trey Seeker

The Blue Whale

The big blue whale swims
It lives in the blue ocean
It swims deep down

Julian O'steen

Elephants

Elephants eat leaves
Elephants play in the mud
I love elephants

Rosalie Howerton

Cheeseburgers

Cheeseburgers have cheese
Sometimes only meat and cheese
It's buns meat and cheese

Luke Whipple

Cheetahs

Look how fast they are
They run around all day long
Cheetahs are big cats

Parker Roberson

Rose Bud

It sways in the breeze
They come in many colors
The petals fly off

Brooklyn Blockberger

Yellow Sun

Look up people see
See the sun waiting up high
The sun shall be shared

Ella Jenkins

Lions

Lions rest on rocks
Lions sleep during the day
Lions hunt at night

Ben Helton

Birds

Birds sing so pretty
Their loud voice is peace to all
Birds are pretty colors

Abby Germaine

Spring Comes Every Year

Flowers need water
Every year spring comes again
The birds sing pretty

Marleah MacLean

Beautiful Trees

Trees stand proud and tall
Look at the leaves and the branches
Pretty in the fall

Shelby Morgan

Robins

Robins are red creatures
They live in a nest in trees
Robins fly in the sky

Jackson Berzsenyi

Leaves Falling

Sun appears in fall
Leaves rustle high in the sky
Now autumn is here

Aneesh Choudhary

Bees in the Breeze

I will hear buzzing
In the way as the bees can
Sip sweet nectar away

Emerson Brown

Lions

They roar very loud
Lions eat meat so do we
Lions live in packs

Aidan Chupp

Sunny Day

A hot sunny day
Go with friends to have some fun
We are all happy

Kayla Williams

Komodo Dragons

Big and strong
Tough and deadly animals
Watch out for them!

Mac Williams

Math

Math is fun so fun
Math is good for learning your numbers
Math is cool for division

Sophia Brown

Collard Greens

They are good to eat
They are very good for you
And they are leafy

Jordan Marshall

My Minecraft

I play on Minecraft
My friends play on Minecraft too
Do you, or do you?

Harper Osburn

Spring

Birds chirp all day long
Little children singing song
That's why I like spring

Zhen Rosemond

At the Pool

At the pool I dive
Cannonball! What a big splash
I had a fun day

Macie Butcher

Playing Outside

I love playing tag!
It is fun to play outside
Try to play some day!

Kiersten Dearing

Baseball

Bats are swinging fast
Baseballs come, people screaming
Pop flies in the air

Luke Sheffield

The Beach

A tropical breeze
Through my wet dirty blond hair
I splash and I play

Noela Rain Kettle

Christmas Magic

Sugar plums floating
The air is sweet and frosty
I shout Christmas' here

Sadie Burleson

The 49ers

Our team is winning
We are winning by one point
Champions, hurray!

James Calhoun

Spaghetti

Spaghetti is neat
It's deliciously awesome
It's the best food made

Rylan Serrano

Golf

My dad loves golfing
My dad teaches me to golf
And I get better

David Hwang

My Birthday

I love my birthday
We go swimming in the pool
All of my friend come

Paige Pearson

Bluebirds

Beautiful bluebirds
They sit on the bird feeder
I love them a lot

Julia Saieg

Missing Fish

Peacefully swimming
Glug, glug, down the drain it goes
"Where is my fish mom?"

Peyton Franks

Seasons

Spring, winter, is joy
Children play outside with joy
After dinner comes

Leyana Moy

The Sun

When it is summer
I like to play in the sun
Sometimes I get burned

Kaydence Ahearn

Minecraft

I can build a lot
I build a diamond castle
Minecraft is so cool

Ben Graf

Science

Science is the best
It's my favorite subject
We're scientists too!

Alana Pablo

Beautiful Northern Lights

Beauty in the sky
In the north of the South Pole
Showing you the way

Corey Menard

My Birthday

I like my birthday
I get fireworks and cake
I have lots of fun

Ben Oberdorfer

Basketball

I dribble the ball
And took the shot and I scored
I had a fun time

Max Davis

Soccer

Soccer is the best!
Cheers are coming really fast!
Then I see the goal!

Abby Tucker

Student Trees

We are student trees
We will grow strong, smart, and big
Thank you Hendricks school!

Charlotte Caccam

Rollerblading

One foot then next foot
Gliding like a bird in flight
Blading is super

Emma Domingo

Summer

Summer is so fun
Sun is beating into grass
I go to the pool!

Lauren Livingston

My Birthday

I jumped out of bed
Mom surprised me with a cake
"Make a wish", mom said

Sofie Lindberg

Summer

Pretty summer beach
Palm trees with sky-blue outlines
I love turquoise waves

Campbell Scharer

Tim Tebow

My name is Tebow
I am the best quarterback
Football is my thing

Boyd Curry

BFF

Sitting and waiting
For my best friend to arrive
I run to sweet heart

Leyton Byrd

Summer

Eating popsicles
Going to the park to play
Having fun all day

Priya Patel

Nutella

Nutella is soft
I eat it all day thank you
Then I go and play

Grace Amato

Reading

Reading is so fun
Yesterday I was reading
A really cool book

Noah Ray

Soccer

I adore soccer
Spring is the time for soccer fun
Soccer is awesome

Ava Byrd

The Explosion

The explosion burst
It looked like fireworks in air
They thought the earth broke

Charlie Reid

Valentine's Day

It is full of hearts
Valentine's Day is closer
It's full of love notes

Trinity Lyons

Minecraft

Blocks are all around
Creeper ready to blow up
Marvelous Minecraft

Mia McLendon

Poje Bear

Furry polar bear
Poje, King of the Artic
Sleeping in my bed

Chace Caven

Winter Days

Crystals in the trees
It is very cold outside
Leaves are falling down

Alexa Dollar

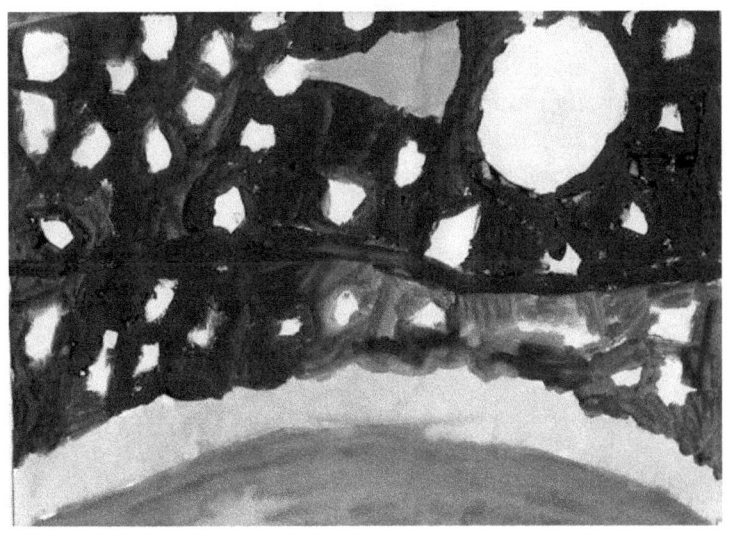

The Moon

Beautiful in sight
Younger sister of the sun
The earth loves the moon

Gretchen Morgan

Magnolia Flower

It sways in the breeze
As I see it flow softly
And the colors wave

Meg Ritter

Robins Fly Up North

Robins fly up north
Every year around this time
May they get home safe

Marleah MacLean

Fourth Grade

 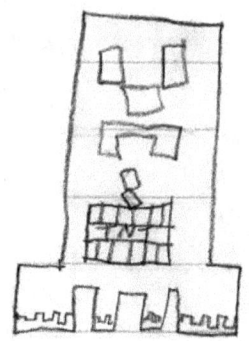

Minecraft

I just love Minecraft
But I hate the Creepers, man
But I love Minecraft

Alexis Walker

Komodo Dragons

Komodo islands
Super dangerous watch out
Awesome komodos!

Sheridan Cheshire

Lizards

Seen mostly in fall
Lizards can get very big
Beautiful lizards

Simon Dichiara

Wind

Over land and sea
Hearing, feeling, not seeing
What is this weird thing?

Tommy Rossi

Pandas

Seen in summer days
Bright colors in the bright sun
Colorful pandas

Jinghai Qiu

Seattle Seahawks

Champion games
Seattle Seahawks are great
They're my favorite

Antraveius Baker

Soothing Sunset

Beautiful sunset
Wind brushes against my face
Moon is shining bright

Claire Aho

Dance Star

Tap shoes click clack click!
Ballerinas scatter!
Hip Hop dancers pop!

Jalyn Leggett

FIFA Soccer 13

L.A. Galaxy
Juke, pass, shoot, deflected... SCORE!
Landon Donovan

Griffin Noel

Rainbow

Colors fill the sky
Makes the dark skies go away
It's a pretty day

Leah Troup

Snow

Cold snowflakes
White little animals
Cold winter fun snow

Kaleb Hinchliffe

Wind Chimes

Heard on windy days
Makes your heart sing happily
Beautiful wind chimes

Patrick Smith

My Baby Bro

He's silly and fun
Playful, quick, little, stinker
Big truck adorer

Griffin Noel

Bears

Seen in summer days
Bears are often seen in summer
Hot and sweaty bears

Alic Popera

Monkeys

Monkeys are funny
Bananas are so yummy
I so love monkeys

Mallory Jones

Snow Flakes

Gently falling
On a blanket that is snow
On the soft brown ground

Lily Pecnik

Legos

I enjoy Legos
Wonderful, colorful toys
Endless fun for me

Brian Wilkes

The Fox

A fluffy red coat
Adorable, fuzzy tail
Bright eyes stare at me

Gillian Snowden-Duguid

Soccer

Lionel Messi
Futbol club Barcelona
Miami Fusion

Ashton Gillis

Unicorns

Their sparkly horn
Galloping in the meadow
They fly on rainbows

Ashlin Elson

Yummy Spaghetti

Spaghetti yum, yum
The sauce and the parmesan cheese
I savor the taste

Hailee Papa

Sunset

Beautiful sunsets
Colors glisten in the sky
Bye day, hello night

Lauren Holland

Sox

Sox - funny, crazy
Sox - scared, annoying, and cute
Sox - has soft black fur

Madeline Chadbourne

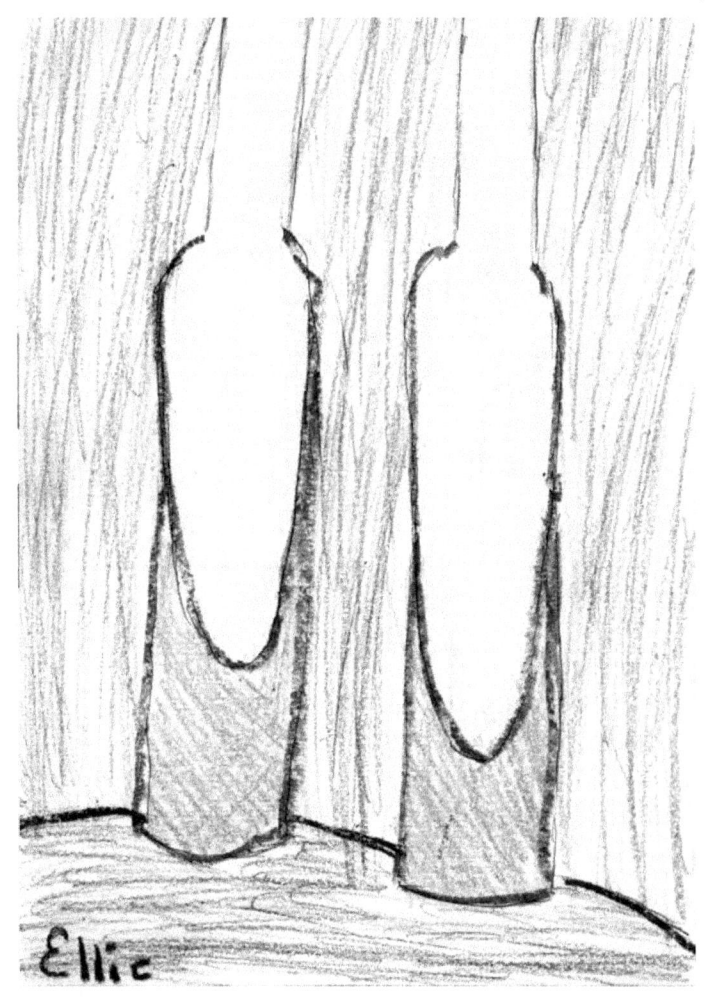

My Life Love

Step, step, step point flex
Hope fills me up when I do
I love to dance, A LOT!

Ellie G.

DANCING

Dancing is so fun
Hear the tap shoes click, click, click
Dancing really ROCKS!

Justice Johnson

The Diamond

I see a diamond
It's shiny with lots of gems
That is why I mine

Horatio Gilman

The Arctic Wolf

Arctic wolf fresh white
Tromping through the wet white snow
Eyes glisten yellow

Reagan McDaniel

The Freezing Winter

The freezing winter
Snow falling elegantly
It's sensational

Sam Davis

The Champions FSU

Go FSU go
Champions will win the game
FSU will win

Clayton Huffman

Pigs

Pink pigs are chubby
Adorable pigs are cute
Pigs are wonderful

Hallie Spell

Mr. "M" Man

Please, sir, mi-mister
Please give me back my dime, sir
For this dime is mine

Kaelin Ensor

Ballerina My Cat

White soft fuzzy fur
Silently sleeping on me
My wonderful cat

Madison Elise Germany

Watch Out!

Poisonous mushrooms
How vivid their colors seen
Don't touch mother scolds

Nathan Mark Shad

Ice Cream

Ice cream is yummy
There are good flavors to eat
I love my ice cream

John Nikolis Acampora

Brothers

Brothers are so fun
Brothers can be annoying
I love my brothers

Will Brandler

Hendricks is the Best

Hendricks is the best
The best in the whole world yup!
Yes it is it is

Skylar Totty

Gummy Bears

Squishy and chewy
Variety of colors
I love gummy bears

Kelsey Kettel

Cats and Dogs

Cats are really cool
Dogs are awesome like cats too
Dogs and cats both rock

Tatum Bowen

Olympics

One every two years
We have winter and summer
Olympics are here

David Tarbox

The FLOWER

Flowers bloom daily
They bask in the warm sunshine
I love the flower

Emily Lombana

Alice, the Dog

Alice, short brown fur
Alice, happy and playful
Alice, the best dog

Jolie K. Dresner

Beach Days!

Sparkling water
Sand creeping between my toes
I adore beach days

Mary Andrews

Ice Cream

Ice cream, ice cream who
Summer days are just so cool
Ice cream, ice cream who

Carter McKee

Lollipops

Sweet candy of mine
Not sticky but has a stick
Awesome lollipops

Orion Hocking

Hello

How are you, hello?
Hello, how are you buddy?
What is the problem?

Tyrell Mitchell

Baseball

Swing goes the batter
Crack goes the sound of the bat
But I catch the ball

Johnny Vodenicker

Coconuts

In the real hot air
There are big old coconuts
Brown as a grizzly bear

Maddox Mills

Winter

Significant skies
Softly howling, frosty winds
Winter snow all day

Max Griffin

Sweet Builds

Oh, big cool great builds,
Oh, the great fun Minecraft
Oh, what build you do

Sebastian Ruiz-Aldana

Peanut Butter

Peanut butter yes
My favorite food that is right
Peanut butter love

Ayden Boone

All About Me

This is me, all me
Pretty, beautiful, and smart
Pretty awesome right

Autumn Higgins

Peanut Butter Cup

Peanut butter cup
Peanut butter in a cup
Very delicious

Julianna Rimondi

The Pond

Croaking frogs on pads
Sunshine warmed fish in aqua
The beautiful pond

Andrew Pearson

The Smoking Civil War

Loud, scary, brave
Smoking shots with a big bang
The big Civil war

Asher Olive-Hall

Light in Darkness

The light in darkness
Signals lots of hope for good
It glistens with life

Coben Balch

That is Me

Fun, happy, playful
Helpful and happy again
That is me, all me

Deama Safar

The Giants Baseball Game

The had won the game
The Giants had won the score
It was a great time

Tyrese Mitchell

Camping

In the fall I camp
I get to roast marshmallows
I don't want to leave

Charlie and Philip Locke

Zip, Zap, Pip, Pop

Pip, pap, zip, zap, BOOM!
Lightning goes pip pop zip zap
The thunder goes boom

Ethan Edwards

The Best NFL Games

I love football games
I saw Joe Flacco play games
I like the Ravens

Zion Vernon

The Blue Dark Sea

The blue shining sea
The sea is cold and silver
The sea is my dream

Alana Dor

Dogs

Dogs are loving pets
You should care for pets like dogs
Dogs are the best pets

Violet Leuthold

Nick Marshall

Nick Marshall is quick
Nick Marshall played for Auburn
Nick Marshall is cool

Henry Jackson

NBA Blacktop

Lebron is a beast
Kevin Durant is better
Derrick Rose is a boss

Adam Waller

Flyers in the Sky

Flyers in the sky
Sharp talon in the sky why?
To hunt in the sky

Emmanuel Orr

Starry Night!

Stars in the tonight
They shine in the starry world
Shines in tomorrow

Mayson Wilkins

DOGS

Arf, arf goes my dog
Dogs are caring and loving
You should care for them

Payton McLendon

NBA Ballers

Carmelo is a boss
Kevin Durant is better
Lebron is a beast

Jakie Judge

Beautiful Colorful Butterflies

They are beautiful
They are the most colorful
I love butterflies

Anaiah Glass

Exotic Flowers

Exotic flowers
Put in beautiful vases
They make my heart shine

Campbell Miller

Purple

Purple is a color
Purple can be a friend
I love purple

Julianna Rimondi

Night Sky

It was dead silent
Stars were glistening in the sky
The moon shining bright

Laci Mickler

The Football Games

Seen in your backyard
Zoom past your face like a car
Struck in your hands fast

Jack Damon

Showstopper

It's all about me
The fun Showstopper is now
I won a medal

Zoe Joyce

Tigers

Whitened, red tigers
Vicious, aggressive tigers
Sharp, clawing tigers

Andrew Harbin

Summer

The summer breeze blows
Water crashes down on shore
The blazing hot sun

Grace Frazier

Purple Petals

Purple petals dance
Purple petals fall softly
Purple petals grow

Sofia Chepenik

Flowers

Pink, silky flowers
Glisten in the afternoon
Silently speaking

Rian Pablo

Mountain Stream

A beautiful stream
Cascades over mountain rocks
Cool and crystal clear

Joseph Poole

Katniss Everdeen

I'm Katniss Everdeen
I am the girl on fire
I won the games twice

Andromeda Makros

Camping

Setting up the tent
In the beautiful nature
Look at the raccoon

Jessica Malosh

Snow

Seen in the arctic
Covers the ground in a blanket
Might build a snowman

Kelly Rose

Tae Kwon Do

Tae kwon do is cool
There is kicking and punching
I like breaking boards

Brock St. Denis

Peace

Peace is wonderful
Peace is a letter to God
Peace calms me any time

Hallie Spell

Fifth Grade

Minecraft

Minecraft is awesome
It is really fun to play
You should play it too

Hayley Connor

Super Bowl XLVIII

Two teams came to win
Seahawks, Broncos, watch them play
A total blowout!

Ethan Elkins

The Secret Soldier

The Secret Soldier
Is really interesting
And a good novel

Zaria Wilson

Tulips

Pink tulip petals
Growing in your window box
Fill my heart with joy!

Emily Singleton

What My Weird Little Brother Said

"Ah, be, bop bo beep!"
My weird little brother said
"Grunt shiyah wah wah!"

Sam Helmick

Dogs

They are very brave
As fast as eagles
Like to bark very loud

Evan Field

Recess

Recess is awesome
You can play so many games
And have loads of fun

Henry Hunter

Diamonds, Diamonds Everywhere

Diamonds everywhere
Diamonds glisten and stare and
I found a diamond in you

Nadia Niang

My School

Hendricks Avenue
I have been here four 6 years
I will miss this school

Alexis Foster

Friends

Friends are made for hugs
Hugs make me feel wonderful
We play together

Mary Woodword

Which is Better?

Minecraft, I do love
My Little Pony rocks too
It's so hard to choose

Lyric Etienne

Haikus

Haikus have seven
Syllables in the middle
Five up and five down

Artin X. Rezaei

Horses

Flowing manes and tails
I love the pretty horses
Trotting through my mind

Ashley Nelson

Peace

Grudges lead to war
Peace brings unity to all
Which do you prefer?

Alex Drew

Island of Misfit Toys

I'm not broken yet
But you still can't fix me, see
Just a misfit toy

Alea Farah

Big Bang Theory

Big Bang Theory
Penny, Leonard, Amy
They are all funny

Lydia-Rose Hanson

Sushi

California roll
A delicious treat it is
Come try it today

Makayla Vath

Pandas

Pandas, Pandas, how
Wonderful they are! So sweet
With love! Pandas! Yay!

Aishea Aliwalas

Legos

One brick at a time
I create a tiny town
Building with Legos

Blake Caven

Flower

Flower gleam and gold
Flower let me see your shine
Magic is now mine

Melanie Jimenez

Things I Love To Do

I love to sing songs
It is fun to dance with friends
I like to swim too

Maisy Webber

The Deer

The deer is silent
Her fawn prances gracefully
I keep my distance

Ashley Shakib

A Singing Life

A singing life's great
Many love to have a voice
A beautiful voice

YG Popera

Minecraft

Mining and building
Survival or creative?
Minecraft is the best!

Zoe Sierra

Games

Games are exiting
Games are adventure and fun
Games are the champ boss

Michele Wang

Flowers

Sweet smelling flowers
Growing on the ends of stems
Flowers everywhere!

Augustina Cole

Technology

Technology rules
Minecraft, Kodu, and more games
Electronics rock

Jack Ferguson

Green

Green is nature's theme
It's the color of mountains
In the summer time

Robert Ritchie

Koala Bears

Koala bears are gray
Koala bears like to climb trees
Koala bears eat leaves

Gabe Singleton

Beach

Cool ocean breeze
Brushing my skin
Sun shining bright

Jake Murphy

Middle School

Exciting, scary
I will miss here, all teachers
Sad but excited

Reagan Burleson

Dolphins

Swim in the water
You'll see them fly in water
You can see them now

Nina Johnson

Dalmatians

Live in a station
Alarm sounds, they respond to call
Dalmatians do it all

Brooke Daly

Life

I see light and hope
Beautiful colors and sounds
I see and hear LIFE

Olivia Pecora

My Last Year

Middle school is next
I've seen all the years pass by
Good bye everyone

Jo'Elle Copeland

Football is Awesome

Football is great fun
I love it and so should you
So go play football

Justin Farhat

All Sport

Hit the ball all hard
Dribble, dribble, shoot the ball
Pass it to me now

Jacob Ritchie

Sharks

Shark, Shark teeth so sharp!
He's swimming down the sea shore
Swimming sleek sharp sharks!

William Berry

Amazing World

Mossy rocks in the water
Beautiful blue skies above
My amazing world

Emma Molenaar

Dragons

Dragons are mighty
Dragons are rare to be seen
The dragon's scales shine

Carson Dell'Alba

Colorful

They bloom with delight
All the petals open up
A burst of color

Kate Rogers

Golf

Birds chirping all day
The little white ball flying
Through the air in golf

Will Davis

Basketball

Dribble the ball fast
Pass it to your left or right
Or hit the basket

Kate Isaac

Betta

Beautiful orange, blue
Swims so slow and angelic
The small fish Simon

Caroline Jones

Famous Jameis

The Heisman winner
National Champs, Triple Crown
Most well known freshman

Austin Franks

Football

Down, set, hike, hike, hike
Go deep, I'll throw you the ball
Yay you caught the ball

Cooper Hayman

The Game

Pass it in
Dribble it down
Put it up and in the hoop

Reagan Sheffield

The Sea Temple

The invisible
The mythical place of peace
The serene temple

Spencer Hodge

Manatees

Peaceful manatees
Silently swimming all day
What graceful creatures

Davis Ellis

Sports

Football and baseball
Catching, kicking, throwing fun!
Sports and athletes rock!

West Allred

Surfs Up

The nice blue ocean
Waves crashing on to the beach
Makes me want to surf

Nick Snyder

Henry the Eagle

Henry the Eagle
Flying so high in the sky
How free you must feel

Jacob Cook

Singin Fun

There was one red bird
There was one singin blue bird
And they were singing together

Brooks Berry

Ode to My Cat Shoes

My cat shoes are white
They cats have rockstar glasses
I will wear them soon

Gracie Filmont

LOVELY

She loves to say hi
With her pink tongue flying hi
She is a dog - say hi!

Matteo Turra

The Scary House

There's a scary house
Vampires, Zombies, and Ghosts
Get me out of here

Andreus Chrisman

Tacos

Tacos are awesome
Tacos found at Taco Bell
they have lots of cheese

Joshua Hardin

Mockingjay You Tweet

Mockingjay, you tweet
I love your intriguing sound
So beautifully

Madeline Davis

Sports

I love playing sports
I can't find my favorite
Maybe football is

Jack Bogan

Faculty and Staff

Switch

Three way switch is fun
Are Beyer, Riska, Patsy
Having all the fun?

Craig Beyer

My Library

Shelves filled with good books
Peaceful, quiet place to read
Takes me anywhere

Susan Wilkes

The Beach

Ocean breeze on me
Sunshine touching my brown skin
The beach is my friend

Ms. Henderson

Haiku Logic

Haikus are the best
There are times they don't make sense
Georgia Bulldogs rule!

Andrew Hurst

Room 103

Busy as bees
As fun as clowns in a show
Our kids are bright stars!

Tracy Langley

Bookkeeper Lady

Numbers are my game
Payrolls, checks, vouchers and more
Bookkeeper that's me!

Kate Hurst

LOTS

LOTS do so much work
Mary Woodward is my LOT
I will miss her tons

Mr. Beyer

Ode to 5th Grade Students

My students are cool
All of them are quite unique
5th grade students ROCK!

Craig Beyer

Grandbabies

Children, only 3
Grandbabies, 3 boys, 2 girls
1 happy grammy

Jane Moore

This is Me!

Registrar my gig
Genesis my nemesis
Numbers make me nuts

Mary Pat Innis

Mrs. Riska's Class

Mrs. Riska's class
Lunch bunch, good news, class meetings
Mrs. Riska's class

Joanne Riska

Daughters

Two sweet girls to love
Hugs and kisses everyday
Life is oh so sweet

Mrs. Halter

Rose

Bright color fusion
Pleasant fragrance floats freely
Bold statement of faith

Christina MacDowell

Life's Doors

Life's doors open wide
Broad, narrow, runway for sure
Your personal choice

Rose Hanson

Spaghetti

Oh my spaghetti
I dream about you day and night
What a fun delight

Mr. Federico

The Opening

Control the center
Next, develop your pieces
Castling is good

George Foote

Beach

Brilliant, warm sunshine
Softly roaring clear blue waves
The beach beckons me!

Mrs. Allred

Fourth Graders

Grow into greatness
Fourth grade morphing into fifth
We love fourth graders!

Ms. Shakib

Landon

He has big blue eyes
Crawling around all day long
Saying da-da-da!

Mrs. Healy

www.ingramcontent.com/pod-product-compliance
Lightning Source LLC
Chambersburg PA
CBHW070643050426
42451CB00008B/278